DISNEP · PIXAR

by Mickie Matheis

THE INCREDIBLES

MAD LIBS®

Mad Libs
An imprint of Penguin Random House

MAD LIBS
Penguin Young Readers Group
An Imprint of Penguin Random House LLC

Mad Libs format copyright © 2018 by Penguin Random House LLC. All rights reserved.

Concept created by Roger Price & Leonard Stern

Copyright © 2018 Disney Enterprises, Inc and Pixar.

Published by Mad Libs,
an imprint of Penguin Random House LLC,
345 Hudson Street, New York, New York 10014.
Printed in the USA.

ISBN 9781524787141
1 3 5 7 9 10 8 6 4 2

MAD LIBS

INSTRUCTIONS

MAD LIBS® is a game for people who don't like games!
It can be played by one, two, three, four, or forty.

• RIDICULOUSLY SIMPLE DIRECTIONS

In this tablet you will find stories containing blank spaces where words
are left out. One player, the READER, selects one of these stories. The
READER does not tell anyone what the story is about. Instead, he/she asks
the other players, the WRITERS, to give him/her words. These words are
used to fill in the blank spaces in the story.

• TO PLAY

The READER asks each WRITER in turn to call out a word—an adjective or
a noun or whatever the space calls for—and uses them to fill in the blank
spaces in the story. The result is a MAD LIBS® game.

When the READER then reads the completed MAD LIBS® game to the other
players, they will discover that they have written a story that is fantastic,
screamingly funny, shocking, silly, crazy, or just plain dumb—depending
upon which words each WRITER called out.

• EXAMPLE (*Before* and *After*)

"_____!" he said _____
      EXCLAMATION   ADVERB

as he jumped into his convertible _____ and
                                             NOUN

drove off with his _____ wife.
                           ADJECTIVE

"_____**OUCH**_____!" he said _____**STUPIDLY**_____
      EXCLAMATION   ADVERB

as he jumped into his convertible _____**CAT**_____ and
                                             NOUN

drove off with his _____**BRAVE**_____ wife.
                           ADJECTIVE

MAD LIBS®
QUICK REVIEW

In case you have forgotten what adjectives, adverbs, nouns, and verbs are, here is a quick review:

An ADJECTIVE describes something or somebody. *Lumpy, soft, ugly, messy,* and *short* are adjectives.

An ADVERB tells how something is done. It modifies a verb and usually ends in "ly." *Modestly, stupidly, greedily,* and *carefully* are adverbs.

A NOUN is the name of a person, place, or thing. *Sidewalk, umbrella, bridle, bathtub,* and *nose* are nouns.

A VERB is an action word. *Run, pitch, jump,* and *swim* are verbs. Put the verbs in past tense if the directions say PAST TENSE. *Ran, pitched, jumped,* and *swam* are verbs in the past tense.

When we ask for A PLACE, we mean any sort of place: a country or city (*Spain, Cleveland*) or a room (*bathroom, kitchen*).

An EXCLAMATION or SILLY WORD is any sort of funny sound, gasp, grunt, or outcry, like *Wow!, Ouch!, Whomp!, Ick!,* and *Gadzooks!*

When we ask for specific words, like a NUMBER, a COLOR, an ANIMAL, or a PART OF THE BODY, we mean a word that is one of those things, like *seven, blue, horse,* or *head.*

When we ask for a PLURAL, it means more than one. For example, *cat* pluralized is *cats.*

MAD LIBS® is fun to play with friends, but you can also play it by yourself! To begin with, DO NOT look at the story on the page below. Fill in the blanks on this page with the words called for. Then, using the words you have selected, fill in the blank spaces in the story.

Now you've created your own hilarious MAD LIBS® game!

HEROES
THROUGHOUT HISTORY

A PLACE _____

ADJECTIVE _____

VERB _____

VERB ENDING IN "ING" _____

PLURAL NOUN _____

NOUN _____

ANIMAL _____

NUMBER _____

NOUN _____

TYPE OF LIQUID _____

PLURAL NOUN _____

PLURAL NOUN _____

PART OF THE BODY (PLURAL) _____

ADJECTIVE _____

PERSON IN ROOM _____

NOUN _____

ANIMAL _____

CELEBRITY _____

MAD LIBS
HEROES
THROUGHOUT HISTORY

During the Golden Age of Superheroes, (the) _____ was a
                                             A PLACE

safe, _____ place to live and _____. There were
         ADJECTIVE   VERB

Supers _____ around every corner, ready to save the
         VERB ENDING IN "ING"

day from bad _____. These _____-fighting
                 PLURAL NOUN   NOUN

characters included:

- **Mr. Incredible:** As strong as a/an _____, he could
                                           ANIMAL

  single-handedly lift a/an _____-ton _____.
                               NUMBER   NOUN

- **Frozone:** Able to freeze _____ and create slippery
                                 TYPE OF LIQUID

  _____.
     PLURAL NOUN

- **Gazerbeam:** Could generate deadly laser _____ from
                                                PLURAL NOUN

  his _____.
       PART OF THE BODY (PLURAL)

- **Elastigirl:** Had a super stretchy, _____ body that
                                            ADJECTIVE

  could become any shape or size.

- _____: A lesser-known Super who could transform
    PERSON IN ROOM

  into anything, like a/an _____, a/an _____,
                             NOUN   ANIMAL

  or even _____.
             CELEBRITY

MAD LIBS® is fun to play with friends, but you can also play it by yourself! To begin with, DO NOT look at the story on the page below. Fill in the blanks on this page with the words called for. Then, using the words you have selected, fill in the blank spaces in the story.

Now you've created your own hilarious MAD LIBS® game!

ONE SUPER FAMILY

ADJECTIVE _____

PART OF THE BODY _____

A PLACE _____

VERB ENDING IN "ING" _____

PERSON IN ROOM (FEMALE) _____

VERB ENDING IN "ING" _____

PLURAL NOUN _____

CELEBRITY (MALE) _____

ADJECTIVE _____

NOUN _____

VERB _____

SILLY WORD _____

NOUN _____

NOUN _____

ADJECTIVE _____

ONE SUPER FAMILY

Bob Parr, known during his Superhero days as Mr. _____,
                                                    ADJECTIVE

really misses the _____-racing excitement of fighting
                    PART OF THE BODY

crime. He wants to be out saving (the) _____, not
                                          A PLACE

_____ at a desk in an office from 9:00 a.m. to
VERB ENDING IN "ING"

5:00 p.m. every day. His wife, _____, aka Elastigirl,
                                PERSON IN ROOM (FEMALE)

has adjusted to civilian life better. She doesn't mind doing ordinary

things like laundry, vacuuming, or _____. She also
                                      VERB ENDING IN "ING"

enjoys raising their three young _____, Violet, Dash, and
                                    PLURAL NOUN

baby _____, to be just like everyone else. Bob wishes
      CELEBRITY (MALE)

the children could show off their _____ powers. For example,
                                    ADJECTIVE

Dash could easily be the star of the school's _____-ball team
                                                NOUN

if he was allowed to use his super speed to _____ as fast as he
                                              VERB

could. But his mother won't let him. _____! Saving people
                                        SILLY WORD

from a burning _____ or a runaway _____ is hard
                  NOUN   NOUN

work indeed, but so is raising a/an _____ family!
                                      ADJECTIVE

MAD LIBS® is fun to play with friends, but you can also play it by yourself! To begin with, DO NOT look at the story on the page below. Fill in the blanks on this page with the words called for. Then, using the words you have selected, fill in the blank spaces in the story.

Now you've created your own hilarious MAD LIBS® game!

MY VERY OWN
EDNA MODE

ARTICLE OF CLOTHING _____

NOUN _____

PERSON IN ROOM _____

A PLACE _____

ADJECTIVE _____

PLURAL NOUN _____

ADJECTIVE _____

VERB ENDING IN "ING" _____

NOUN _____

ADJECTIVE _____

PART OF THE BODY _____

COLOR _____

PLURAL NOUN _____

VERB ENDING IN "ING" _____

ANIMAL (PLURAL) _____

VERB _____

I just learned that I am getting a Super-_____
                                        ARTICLE OF CLOTHING

made by Edna Mode, _____ designer extraordinaire! Her
                        NOUN

client list contains some of the biggest names in Superherodom, like

Mr. Incredible, Elastigirl, Frozone, _____, and many
                                      PERSON IN ROOM

others from around (the) _____. Edna has become
                              A PLACE

somewhat of a Superhero herself, creating amazingly _____
                                                      ADJECTIVE

custom designs using the best fabrics, state-of-the-art technology, and

hard to find _____. Edna's office had me fill out this
                PLURAL NOUN

questionnaire to ensure she designs an outfit that lets me fully use

my _____-powers and look stylish while doing it.
      ADJECTIVE

- My Super power is high-speed _____, which means
                                 VERB ENDING IN "ING"

  I need a/an _____-based fabric that withstands friction.
                  NOUN

- I think my best feature is my _____ _____.
                                  ADJECTIVE   PART OF THE BODY

- If I could choose any print to put on my suit, it would be either

_____ _____ or _____
      COLOR   PLURAL NOUN   VERB ENDING IN "ING"

_____.
  ANIMAL (PLURAL)

I am so excited, I can hardly _____!
                                VERB

MAD LIBS® is fun to play with friends, but you can also play it by yourself! To begin with, DO NOT look at the story on the page below. Fill in the blanks on this page with the words called for. Then, using the words you have selected, fill in the blank spaces in the story.

Now you've created your own hilarious MAD LIBS® game!

ODE TO THE SUPERS

ADJECTIVE _____

ARTICLE OF CLOTHING (PLURAL) _____

PLURAL NOUN _____

PERSON IN ROOM _____

A PLACE _____

ANIMAL _____

ADJECTIVE _____

NOUN _____

PLURAL NOUN _____

VERB ENDING IN "ING" _____

PART OF THE BODY _____

SILLY WORD _____

A PLACE _____

ODE TO THE SUPERS

The Golden Age of Superheroes was a/an _____ and glorious time.
ADJECTIVE

Supers in signature _____ spent long days
ARTICLE OF CLOTHING (PLURAL)

fighting crime.

They'd catch sneaky robbers who'd stolen millions

of _____ from a bank.
PLURAL NOUN

They'd stop the evil _____ from attacking
PERSON IN ROOM

(the) _____ with a tank.
A PLACE

They'd take time to rescue a pet _____ stranded
ANIMAL

in a/an _____ tree.
ADJECTIVE

They'd save a runaway _____ from plunging
NOUN

off a bridge into the sea.

When criminals and evil-_____ start to cause some trouble,
PLURAL NOUN

you can bet those trusty Supers will come _____
VERB ENDING IN "ING"

on the double!

So shake a Super's _____ today with a smile on your face,
PART OF THE BODY

and say, "Thanks!" or "_____!" for keeping
SILLY WORD

(the) _____ a safe place.
A PLACE

MAD LIBS® is fun to play with friends, but you can also play it by yourself! To begin with, DO NOT look at the story on the page below. Fill in the blanks on this page with the words called for. Then, using the words you have selected, fill in the blank spaces in the story.

Now you've created your own hilarious MAD LIBS® game!

A MUCH-NEEDED VACATION

VERB ENDING IN "ING" _____

PLURAL NOUN _____

ARTICLE OF CLOTHING (PLURAL) _____

VERB _____

NOUN _____

ADJECTIVE _____

A PLACE _____

NOUN _____

TYPE OF LIQUID _____

PLURAL NOUN _____

VERB ENDING IN "ING" _____

ADJECTIVE _____

ANIMAL _____

ADJECTIVE _____

CELEBRITY _____

PART OF THE BODY _____

You've been _____ very hard for the past several
_____
VERB ENDING IN "ING"

months, trying to save the world. But even Super-_____
_____
PLURAL NOUN

need a vacation. Kick off your _____ and come
_____
ARTICLE OF CLOTHING (PLURAL)

relax and _____ at the Superhero Spa and Suites, a five-
_____
VERB

_____ luxury resort located on the _____ shores
_____   _____
NOUN   ADJECTIVE

of (the) _____. This exclusive oceanfront _____
_____   _____
A PLACE   NOUN

has everything a weary Superhero could ask for in a vacation destination.

Start your day with a cup of steaming hot _____ on your
_____
TYPE OF LIQUID

private patio with breathtaking views of _____, then you
_____
PLURAL NOUN

can head to the beach. One of the most popular activities at the resort

is underwater _____, which lets you get up close and
_____
VERB ENDING IN "ING"

_____ with the many aquatic creatures native to the area,
_____
ADJECTIVE

such as the delicate sea-_____. After a day of fun in the sun,
_____
ANIMAL

return to the resort for a deliciously _____ five-course meal
_____
ADJECTIVE

prepared by our popular chef, _____. The only thing you'll
_____
CELEBRITY

need to save while on your vacation is room in your _____
_____
PART OF THE BODY

for dessert!

MAD LIBS® is fun to play with friends, but you can also play it by yourself! To begin with, DO NOT look at the story on the page below. Fill in the blanks on this page with the words called for. Then, using the words you have selected, fill in the blank spaces in the story.

Now you've created your own hilarious MAD LIBS® game!

CHILLIN' WITH FROZONE

ADJECTIVE _____

PLURAL NOUN _____

PART OF THE BODY (PLURAL) _____

NOUN _____

TYPE OF FOOD _____

ADJECTIVE _____

VERB ENDING IN "ING" _____

CELEBRITY _____

PERSON IN ROOM _____

VERB _____

ADJECTIVE _____

VERB ENDING IN "ING" _____

PART OF THE BODY _____

CHILLIN' WITH FROZONE

Frozone is a/an _____, warmhearted Super whose powers,
         ADJECTIVE

creating icy _____ and freezing surfaces with his
        PLURAL NOUN

_____, make him a fun _____ to be
PART OF THE BODY (PLURAL)   NOUN

around. He can use his frosty fingers to:

- Whip up a/an _____-flavored snow cone at your
           TYPE OF FOOD

  request

- Freeze roads so that school is canceled, which means sleeping

  late and no _____ homework
          ADJECTIVE

- Make an ice-_____ rink right in the middle of
          VERB ENDING IN "ING"

  your yard

- Create dazzling ice sculptures that look like _____ or
             CELEBRITY

  _____
  PERSON IN ROOM

- Fashion a frozen playground in your living room so you can

  swing, slide, and _____
          VERB

- Freeze a patch of ice where the _____ neighborhood
          ADJECTIVE

  bully is _____ so he slips and falls on his
        VERB ENDING IN "ING"

  _____
  PART OF THE BODY

MAD LIBS® is fun to play with friends, but you can also play it by yourself! To begin with, DO NOT look at the story on the page below. Fill in the blanks on this page with the words called for. Then, using the words you have selected, fill in the blank spaces in the story.

Now you've created your own hilarious MAD LIBS® game!

DASH AND VIOLET

ADJECTIVE _____

VERB _____

PLURAL NOUN _____

PERSON IN ROOM (MALE) _____

NOUN _____

ADJECTIVE _____

PART OF THE BODY _____

VERB ENDING IN "ING" _____

ADJECTIVE _____

CELEBRITY (FEMALE) _____

SILLY WORD _____

PART OF THE BODY (PLURAL) _____

CELEBRITY (MALE) _____

PLURAL NOUN _____

NOUN _____

DASH AND VIOLET

Living in a household full of Supers is never dull. Dash and Violet Parr

are like any other _____ siblings—they argue, they bicker,

ADJECTIVE

they _____. It's when they start to use their Super-

VERB

_____ that things get interesting! For example, Violet

PLURAL NOUN

doesn't like when Dash teases her about _____, the

PERSON IN ROOM (MALE)

cute _____ in school she likes. And she really doesn't like

NOUN

when her _____ brother snaps the headband she wears on

ADJECTIVE

her _____ to hold back her hair. He takes off

PART OF THE BODY

_____, leaving her no choice but to conjure up a/an

VERB ENDING IN "ING"

_____ force field for him to run right into. It is usually at

ADJECTIVE

that point when their mother, _____, yells,

CELEBRITY (FEMALE)

"_____!" and uses her super stretchy _____

SILLY WORD — PART OF THE BODY (PLURAL)

to reach out and separate them. Their little brother, _____,

CELEBRITY (MALE)

just laughs at all the commotion. Even if these two _____

PLURAL NOUN

don't always see eye to _____, they still love each other.

NOUN

MAD LIBS® is fun to play with friends, but you can also play it by yourself! To begin with, DO NOT look at the story on the page below. Fill in the blanks on this page with the words called for. Then, using the words you have selected, fill in the blank spaces in the story.

Now you've created your own hilarious MAD LIBS® game!

SHOWDOWN WITH SYNDROME

FIRST NAME (FEMALE) _____

ADVERB _____

A PLACE _____

NOUN _____

PLURAL NOUN _____

EXCLAMATION _____

PLURAL NOUN _____

PERSON IN ROOM (FEMALE) _____

PART OF THE BODY _____

VERB (PAST TENSE) _____

NOUN _____

ADJECTIVE _____

SILLY WORD _____

PLURAL NOUN _____

ADJECTIVE _____

MAD LIBS
SHOWDOWN
WITH SYNDROME

This is _____ McBlabby with WSPR-TV, reporting live
　　　　FIRST NAME (FEMALE)

on the scene where the Incredibles are teaming up to save a local family

home. They _____ demolished the robots that were destroying
　　　　ADVERB

(the) _____. But now Syndrome is trying to kidnap a baby
　　　A PLACE

_____ that neighbors say is called Jack-Jack. The madman
　　NOUN

just blasted a hole in the roof and is racing skyward toward his jet

using the rocket _____ on his feet. _____!
　　　　PLURAL NOUN　　　　　　　　　　　　　EXCLAMATION

Jack-Jack has just burst into flaming _____ and a panicked
　　　　　　　　　　　　　　　　　PLURAL NOUN

Syndrome has dropped him! Is Jack-Jack a goner? Wait! Mr. Incredible

has thrown _____ into the air to catch the baby.
　　　PERSON IN ROOM (FEMALE)

Whoa! She just shaped her stretchy _____ into a parachute,
　　　　　　　　　　　　　　　　PART OF THE BODY

and they have both _____ safely. Syndrome is shaking
　　　　　　　VERB (PAST TENSE)

his _____ in rage, shouting, "This is not the _____
　　NOUN　　　　　　　　　　　　　　　　　　　　　ADJECTIVE

end!" Mr. Incredible has picked up a car and hurled it toward the jet.

_____! The jet has just exploded. Ladies and _____,
SILLY WORD　　　　　　　　　　　　　　　　　PLURAL NOUN

this family isn't just incredible, they're utterly _____!
　　　　　　　　　　　　　　　　　　　　　ADJECTIVE

MAD LIBS® is fun to play with friends, but you can also play it by yourself! To begin with, DO NOT look at the story on the page below. Fill in the blanks on this page with the words called for. Then, using the words you have selected, fill in the blank spaces in the story.

Now you've created your own hilarious MAD LIBS® game!

WHY THE WORLD NEEDS SUPERS

PLURAL NOUN _____

ADJECTIVE _____

VERB (PAST TENSE) _____

PLURAL NOUN _____

CELEBRITY _____

PLURAL NOUN _____

NOUN _____

NUMBER _____

TYPE OF LIQUID _____

ANIMAL (PLURAL) _____

NOUN _____

A PLACE _____

VERB _____

MAD LIBS
WHY THE WORLD NEEDS SUPERS

It was a sad day in history when Supers were forbidden to do any more

hero work. Let's face it, there are a lot of bad _____ in this
                                              PLURAL NOUN

_____ world, and the Supers _____ very
ADJECTIVE   VERB (PAST TENSE)

hard to keep them in line. When someone swiped _____
                                                PLURAL NOUN

that didn't belong to them, the Supers swooped in to get them back.

When villains like Bomb Voyage or _____ threatened to
                                   CELEBRITY

destroy all the high-rise _____ throughout the city, the
                          PLURAL NOUN

Supers defused the situation. When a derailed passenger _____
                                                        NOUN

was about to plummet _____ feet down into the icy
                     NUMBER

_____ below, the Supers halted it in the nick of time. Citizens
TYPE OF LIQUID

could even count on Supers to rescue their pet _____
                                               ANIMAL (PLURAL)

that had gotten stuck or stranded. Supers prided themselves on making

sure that _____ laws were obeyed, order was maintained,
          NOUN

and peace reigned over (the) _____. How can we begin
                             A PLACE

to _____ without them?
   VERB

MAD LIBS® is fun to play with friends, but you can also play it by yourself! To begin with, DO NOT look at the story on the page below. Fill in the blanks on this page with the words called for. Then, using the words you have selected, fill in the blank spaces in the story.

Now you've created your own hilarious MAD LIBS® game!

CUTE GUY, BY VI

ADJECTIVE _____

NOUN _____

NOUN _____

ADJECTIVE _____

CELEBRITY (MALE) _____

ARTICLE OF CLOTHING _____

CELEBRITY _____

NOUN _____

A PLACE _____

NOUN _____

PERSON IN ROOM (MALE) _____

ADJECTIVE _____

PART OF THE BODY _____

VERB ENDING IN "ING" _____

EXCLAMATION _____

Dear Diary,

Being a teenager is really _____, but being a teen Super-
                              ADJECTIVE

_____ is even harder! There's this really cute _____
     NOUN   NOUN

at my school named Tony, and I like him a lot. He's really popular and

_____—kind of like the _____ of Western
     ADJECTIVE   CELEBRITY (MALE)

Junior High School. Well, guess what? He asked me out! But then duty

called, and I had to change into my Superhero _____ to
                                                ARTICLE OF CLOTHING

help my family fight _____, an evil _____ who
                         CELEBRITY   NOUN

was terrorizing (the) _____. I got stuck babysitting my baby
                          A PLACE

_____, Jack-Jack, while my other brother, _____,
     NOUN   PERSON IN ROOM (MALE)

was having all the fun. I got so _____ that I yanked the mask
                                     ADJECTIVE

off my _____ and threw it on the ground—and Tony saw
          PART OF THE BODY

me! He was so freaked out that he took off _____ as
                                              VERB ENDING IN "ING"

fast as he could. When my dad found out, he had Tony's memory

erased. My crush not only forgot about our date, he forgot about me!

_____! I can save the world, why can't I deal with a crush?
     EXCLAMATION

MAD LIBS® is fun to play with friends, but you can also play it by yourself! To begin with, DO NOT look at the story on the page below. Fill in the blanks on this page with the words called for. Then, using the words you have selected, fill in the blank spaces in the story.

Now you've created your own hilarious MAD LIBS® game!

WINSTON DEAVOR: SUPERS FAN

NOUN _____

ADJECTIVE _____

PLURAL NOUN _____

ADJECTIVE _____

A PLACE _____

PLURAL NOUN _____

CELEBRITY (MALE) _____

CELEBRITY (FEMALE) _____

NOUN _____

PLURAL NOUN _____

ARTICLE OF CLOTHING (PLURAL) _____

PLURAL NOUN _____

ADJECTIVE _____

NOUN _____

VERB _____

VERB ENDING IN "ING" _____

Winston Deavor was an ordinary _____ with a grand,
                                    NOUN

_____ plan. He wanted to make Super-_____
  ADJECTIVE   PLURAL NOUN

legal again, and as a/an _____, wealthy tycoon, he had the
                            ADJECTIVE

resources to make that happen—like important connections all over

(the) _____ and billions of _____ in the bank.
        A PLACE   PLURAL NOUN

He wanted to legalize hero work in honor of his beloved father,

_____, a great supporter of Supers. After Winston and
  CELEBRITY (MALE)

his sister, _____, built up the world-class _____
            CELEBRITY (FEMALE)   NOUN

company, DevTech, he began to locate Supers in hiding. His plan was

to have tiny, powerful _____ sewn inside Super-
                            PLURAL NOUN

_____ to film heroic acts live and up close. This
  ARTICLE OF CLOTHING (PLURAL)

way, _____ all over the world could see the brave acts
        PLURAL NOUN

performed by the Supers, not just the _____ destruction
                                          ADJECTIVE

they sometimes caused when saving the _____. Winston
                                          NOUN

Deavor made a promise that he would not _____ until
                                            VERB

Superheroes had returned to the crime-_____ glory
                                          VERB ENDING IN "ING"

days that he remembered.

MAD LIBS® is fun to play with friends, but you can also play it by yourself! To begin with, DO NOT look at the story on the page below. Fill in the blanks on this page with the words called for. Then, using the words you have selected, fill in the blank spaces in the story.

Now you've created your own hilarious MAD LIBS® game!

VEHICLE MAINTENANCE

VEHICLE _____

TYPE OF LIQUID _____

ADJECTIVE _____

PLURAL NOUN _____

VERB ENDING IN "ING" _____

NOUN _____

NOUN _____

PERSON IN ROOM _____

CELEBRITY _____

VERB _____

VERB ENDING IN "ING" _____

TYPE OF LIQUID _____

PART OF THE BODY _____

Safely operating a Superhero _____, like the Incredibile or
VEHICLE

the Elasticycle, involves a lot of responsibility. The *Superhero Vehicle*

Maintenance Handbook advises owners to:

- Only use premium _____ as fuel because it's
TYPE OF LIQUID

  powerfully _____
ADJECTIVE

- Keep all the _____ fully inflated for maximum
PLURAL NOUN

  speed and efficiency while _____ on the road
VERB ENDING IN "ING"

- Regularly check that the rocket and _____ launchers
NOUN

  are fully functioning

- Ensure that the voice-activation _____ is properly
NOUN

  set up to recognize the commands of specific Superheroes, like

  Mr. Incredible, _____, and _____
PERSON IN ROOM   CELEBRITY

- Test the controls for Automatic Escape-and-_____
VERB

  mode, Self-_____ mode, and Hydro-Pursuit
VERB ENDING IN "ING"

  mode for driving on _____
TYPE OF LIQUID

- Inspect the ejector seats, which are designed to launch you

  _____-first into the air
PART OF THE BODY

MAD LIBS® is fun to play with friends, but you can also play it by yourself! To begin with, DO NOT look at the story on the page below. Fill in the blanks on this page with the words called for. Then, using the words you have selected, fill in the blank spaces in the story.

Now you've created your own hilarious MAD LIBS® game!

BOB'S TO-DO LIST

PERSON IN ROOM _____

SAME PERSON IN ROOM _____

ADJECTIVE _____

TYPE OF FOOD _____

PLURAL NOUN _____

NOUN _____

PART OF THE BODY _____

TYPE OF LIQUID _____

NUMBER _____

VERB _____

ANIMAL _____

CELEBRITY _____

ADJECTIVE _____

PART OF THE BODY _____

ADJECTIVE _____

Hey honey,

Thanks for taking care of Dash, Violet, and _____-
PERSON IN ROOM

_____ while I'm on assignment. Just a few reminders:
SAME PERSON IN ROOM

- Make sure the kids have a/an _____ breakfast, like
  ADJECTIVE

  eggs, waffles, and _____ juice. Please don't let Dash
  TYPE OF FOOD

  just eat a bowl of Sugar _____.
  PLURAL NOUN

- Check that Dash has finished all of his _____ work and
  NOUN

  that he washed his _____ before getting on the bus.
  PART OF THE BODY

- Jack-Jack likes a bottle of warm _____ at _____
  TYPE OF LIQUID   NUMBER

  o'clock. Then put him in his crib to _____—
  VERB

  otherwise, he'll be a cranky little _____.
  ANIMAL

- He'll doze off more quickly if you read his favorite storybook,

  _____ *in the Land of Noddoff.* And please make
  CELEBRITY

  sure his diaper is _____. If it's drooping from his
  ADJECTIVE

  _____, it probably needs changing.
  PART OF THE BODY

You're not just an awesomely _____ dad—you're my hero!
ADJECTIVE

See you soon!

MAD LIBS® is fun to play with friends, but you can also play it by yourself! To begin with, DO NOT look at the story on the page below. Fill in the blanks on this page with the words called for. Then, using the words you have selected, fill in the blank spaces in the story.

Now you've created your own hilarious MAD LIBS® game!

STOP THAT TRAIN!

EXCLAMATION _____

A PLACE _____

PLURAL NOUN _____

NOUN _____

PERSON IN ROOM _____

CELEBRITY _____

NOUN _____

NUMBER _____

VERB (PAST TENSE) _____

PLURAL NOUN _____

ADJECTIVE _____

VERB ENDING IN "ING" _____

NOUN _____

PART OF THE BODY _____

VERB ENDING IN "ING" _____

Disney · PIXAR

THE INCREDIBLES

STOP THAT TRAIN!

_____, today was an exciting day here in
　　EXCLAMATION

(the) _____! A large crowd of _____, including
　　A PLACE　　　　　　　　　　　　　　PLURAL NOUN

my best _____, _____, and I, gathered to be
　　　　　NOUN　　　　PERSON IN ROOM

the first to ride the new Hovertrain. Mayor _____ had just
　　　　　　　　　　　　　　　　　　　　CELEBRITY

cut the ribbon to launch this high-speed _____ when it
　　　　　　　　　　　　　　　　　　　　NOUN

mysteriously started to go backward instead of forward! Luckily,

Elastigirl was nearby and chased after us on her Elasticycle. The

runaway train whipped through the city at _____ miles per
　　　　　　　　　　　　　　　　　　NUMBER

hour. We watched out the windows as Elastigirl _____
　　　　　　　　　　　　　　　　　　　　VERB (PAST TENSE)

as hard as she could, gunning the Elasticycle through tunnels and across

_____. When she got close enough, she flung herself onto
PLURAL NOUN

the train and stretched into a/an _____ parachute to safely
　　　　　　　　　　　　　　ADJECTIVE

stop it. While almost all of the passengers were screaming and

_____, not a single _____ was hurt. I will
VERB ENDING IN "ING"　　　　　NOUN

never forget it! My _____ was _____ as
　　　　　　　PART OF THE BODY　　　　VERB ENDING IN "ING"

fast as that train!

MAD LIBS® is fun to play with friends, but you can also play it by yourself! To begin with, DO NOT look at the story on the page below. Fill in the blanks on this page with the words called for. Then, using the words you have selected, fill in the blank spaces in the story.

Now you've created your own hilarious MAD LIBS® game!

AWESOME POWERS, BABY!

OCCUPATION _____

NOUN _____

ADJECTIVE _____

SILLY WORD _____

NOUN _____

ANIMAL _____

CELEBRITY _____

NOUN _____

COLOR _____

NOUN _____

PART OF THE BODY (PLURAL) _____

PART OF THE BODY _____

VERB _____

PLURAL NOUN _____

VERB ENDING IN "ING" _____

EXCLAMATION _____

ADJECTIVE _____

Bob was a really proud _____ when he discovered that his
                          OCCUPATION

youngest _____, Jack-Jack, had Super powers. And not just
          NOUN

a single power, but many _____ powers! According to the
                          ADJECTIVE

Parrs' good friend, Edna Mode, Jack-Jack is a/an "_____,"
                                                   SILLY WORD

also known as a polymorph, a person that can change into different

forms, like a/an _____, a/an _____, or even
                  NOUN   ANIMAL

_____. In Jack-Jack's case, he can turn into a flaming
  CELEBRITY

_____, or a monstrous _____ _____,
  NOUN   COLOR   NOUN

especially when he is angry. He can also shoot lasers from his

_____ and levitate. Talk about a/an _____-ful
PART OF THE BODY (PLURAL)   PART OF THE BODY

to babysit! And that's not even mentioning his ability to _____
                                                           VERB

through solid surfaces like walls or doors or even _____.
                                                    PLURAL NOUN

One minute he might be _____ in front of you, and
                       VERB ENDING IN "ING"

the next moment—_____—he's _____. Now
                 EXCLAMATION   ADJECTIVE

that's what you call a Super baby!

MAD LIBS® is fun to play with friends, but you can also play it by yourself! To begin with, DO NOT look at the story on the page below. Fill in the blanks on this page with the words called for. Then, using the words you have selected, fill in the blank spaces in the story.

Now you've created your own hilarious MAD LIBS® game!

THE NEXT GENERATION

ADJECTIVE _____

PLURAL NOUN _____

VERB ENDING IN "ING" _____

VERB _____

ANIMAL (PLURAL) _____

PLURAL NOUN _____

PART OF THE BODY (PLURAL) _____

PART OF THE BODY (PLURAL) _____

TYPE OF LIQUID _____

ADJECTIVE _____

VERB _____

ADJECTIVE _____

Elastigirl finally met the next generation of _____
_____ ADJECTIVE
Superheroes. This group of renegade _____ have amazing
_____ PLURAL NOUN
_____ powers and secret identities, but were forced
VERB ENDING IN "ING"
underground to _____ in undisclosed locations for years.
_____ VERB
The team has some powerful members:

- **Voyd** moves people, _____, and _____
  _____ ANIMAL (PLURAL) _____ PLURAL NOUN

  through space with her portals.

- **He-lectrix** electrocutes things with the electrical charges

  coursing through his _____.
  _____ PART OF THE BODY (PLURAL)

- **Krushauer** smashes things using his own two

  _____.
  PART OF THE BODY (PLURAL)

- **Reflux** spews molten _____ like a human volcano.
  _____ TYPE OF LIQUID

These _____, wannabe Supers couldn't believe they got to
_____ ADJECTIVE
_____ in the same room as Elastigirl—the most famously
VERB
_____ of all Supers!
ADJECTIVE

MAD LIBS® is fun to play with friends, but you can also play it by yourself! To begin with, DO NOT look at the story on the page below. Fill in the blanks on this page with the words called for. Then, using the words you have selected, fill in the blank spaces in the story.

Now you've created your own hilarious MAD LIBS® game!

I, THE SCREENSLAVER

PART OF THE BODY _____

A PLACE _____

ADJECTIVE _____

VERB ENDING IN "ING" _____

TYPE OF FOOD _____

ANIMAL _____

PLURAL NOUN _____

ARTICLE OF CLOTHING (PLURAL) _____

ADJECTIVE _____

ADJECTIVE _____

NOUN _____

PERSON IN ROOM _____

PART OF THE BODY (PLURAL) _____

NOUN _____

I, THE SCREENSLAVER

I despise Superheroes with all of my _____. Why? Because
<u>PART OF THE BODY</u>

they keep all the people of (the) _____ weak and
<u>A PLACE</u>

_____! People just sit around helplessly _____
<u>ADJECTIVE</u> <u>VERB ENDING IN "ING"</u>

all day long while technology and Superheroes take care of everything

for them. Can't decide between the _____ burger or the
<u>TYPE OF FOOD</u>

pasta à la _____? No problem—technology will tell you.
<u>ANIMAL</u>

And Superheroes? They're just another way to replace experience with

simulation. People don't use their minds or _____ anymore
<u>PLURAL NOUN</u>

to solve problems. Just because Superheroes have unusual powers, wear

shiny _____, and have _____ names like
<u>ARTICLE OF CLOTHING (PLURAL)</u> <u>ADJECTIVE</u>

Mr. _____, Elasti-_____, or Super _____
<u>ADJECTIVE</u> <u>NOUN</u> <u>PERSON IN ROOM</u>

doesn't mean people should blindly put their lives into Superheroes'

_____ and hope for the best. Someone needs to step
<u>PART OF THE BODY (PLURAL)</u>

up and take control—and I, the Screenslaver, am the perfect

_____ for the job!
<u>NOUN</u>

MAD LIBS® is fun to play with friends, but you can also play it by yourself! To begin with, DO NOT look at the story on the page below. Fill in the blanks on this page with the words called for. Then, using the words you have selected, fill in the blank spaces in the story.

Now you've created your own hilarious MAD LIBS® game!

FROZONE TO THE RESCUE

PLURAL NOUN _____

A PLACE _____

TYPE OF LIQUID _____

ADJECTIVE _____

NOUN _____

VERB ENDING IN "ING" _____

VERB (PAST TENSE) _____

PLURAL NOUN _____

SILLY WORD _____

ADJECTIVE _____

COLOR _____

PLURAL NOUN _____

PART OF THE BODY (PLURAL) _____

PLURAL NOUN _____

Frozone hurried to the Parr home to check on Violet, Dash, and baby

Jack-Jack. It was a good thing that he did because the Screenslaver had

sent some hypnotized _____ to kidnap the kids and bring

PLURAL NOUN

them back to (the) _____. Frozone sprayed a wall of snow

A PLACE

and icy _____ at the _____ intruders to keep

TYPE OF LIQUID ADJECTIVE

them outside, but they quickly ripped the _____ off its

NOUN

hinges and took off _____ through the house. Frozone

VERB ENDING IN "ING"

fought and _____ with all his might. He yelled to the

VERB (PAST TENSE)

kids to get into his car, but one of the bad guys had crushed it into a

crumpled mass of metal, glass, and _____. Just then, the

PLURAL NOUN

Incredibile raced up with a loud _____. The kids dove into

SILLY WORD

it and watched, horrified and _____, as the hypnotized

ADJECTIVE

minions slammed _____ _____ over poor

COLOR PLURAL NOUN

Frozone's _____, sending him into a trance. But the

PART OF THE BODY (PLURAL)

_____ were able to escape, thanks to Frozone—a first-class

PLURAL NOUN

friend and a super *ice* guy.

MAD LIBS® is fun to play with friends, but you can also play it by yourself! To begin with, DO NOT look at the story on the page below. Fill in the blanks on this page with the words called for. Then, using the words you have selected, fill in the blank spaces in the story.

Now you've created your own hilarious MAD LIBS® game!

SUPERS-STAR DESIGNER

ADJECTIVE _____

NOUN _____

VERB ENDING IN "ING" _____

PERSON IN ROOM _____

NOUN _____

ADJECTIVE _____

PLURAL NOUN _____

ARTICLE OF CLOTHING (PLURAL) _____

ARTICLE OF CLOTHING (PLURAL) _____

PLURAL NOUN _____

ADJECTIVE _____

NOUN _____

A PLACE _____

PART OF THE BODY (PLURAL) _____

Small in stature but a/an _____ giant in the fashion world,
                              ADJECTIVE

Edna Mode is a legend in Superhero _____ design. Like
                                          NOUN

many designers, she began her career _____ with
                                         VERB ENDING IN "ING"

Hollywood stars like _____, but quickly grew tired of the
                       PERSON IN ROOM

_____ premieres and _____ parties. Once she
      NOUN   ADJECTIVE

discovered the secret world of Superheroes, she was hooked. She

believed that Super-_____ should *look* good while *doing*
                      PLURAL NOUN

good. Edna was a genius at blending fashion, form, and function—

perfecting bulletproof _____, and flame-
                        ARTICLE OF CLOTHING (PLURAL)

retardant _____, and inventing rocket-
          ARTICLE OF CLOTHING (PLURAL)

propelled _____ in place of capes. (No capes!) Her career
           PLURAL NOUN

soared to _____ new heights when she designed a miniature
           ADJECTIVE

_____ suit for the youngest member of the Incredibles.
         NOUN

Rumor has it she may be developing a children's clothing label called

Auntie Edna. Superhero parents across (the) _____ are
                                              A PLACE

crossing their _____, hoping it's true!
               PART OF THE BODY (PLURAL)

MAD LIBS® is fun to play with friends, but you can also play it by yourself! To begin with, DO NOT look at the story on the page below. Fill in the blanks on this page with the words called for. Then, using the words you have selected, fill in the blank spaces in the story.

Now you've created your own hilarious MAD LIBS® game!

A PHONE CALL FROM SCHOOL

PERSON IN ROOM (FEMALE) _____

VERB _____

NOUN _____

NOUN _____

A PLACE _____

ADJECTIVE _____

PERSON IN ROOM (MALE) _____

PLURAL NOUN _____

VERB _____

PLURAL NOUN _____

NOUN _____

VERB ENDING IN "ING" _____

NUMBER _____

ADJECTIVE _____

Hello, Mr. and Mrs. Parr. My name is _____, and
PERSON IN ROOM (FEMALE)

I'm Dash's math teacher. I wanted to take the time to _____
VERB

today because I am concerned about Dash's grades. While your son is

no doubt the fastest _____ in the school, he has some
NOUN

catching up to do when it comes to his _____ homework.
NOUN

There are math labs held here in (the) _____ every day after
A PLACE

school under the _____ supervision of myself and my
ADJECTIVE

colleague, _____. The older _____ come
PERSON IN ROOM (MALE)   PLURAL NOUN

and _____ with the younger _____ until they
VERB   PLURAL NOUN

understand the different math concepts we are teaching, like fractions,

decimals, and finding the circumference of a/an _____.
NOUN

There are also steps Dash can take at home to improve his skills. For

example, he told me that he spends a lot of time _____
VERB ENDING IN "ING"

when he gets home. I suggested he shorten that by _____
NUMBER

minutes and devote that time to studying math. Dash's performance is

average, but I know he's capable of being _____!
ADJECTIVE

MAD LIBS® is fun to play with friends, but you can also play it by yourself! To begin with, DO NOT look at the story on the page below. Fill in the blanks on this page with the words called for. Then, using the words you have selected, fill in the blank spaces in the story.

Now you've created your own hilarious MAD LIBS® game!

WANTED: A FEW GOOD SUPERHEROES

TYPE OF FOOD (PLURAL) _____

NOUN _____

PART OF THE BODY (PLURAL) _____

ANIMAL _____

NOUN _____

ADJECTIVE _____

A PLACE _____

PLURAL NOUN _____

VERB ENDING IN "ING" _____

VERB _____

ADJECTIVE _____

ADJECTIVE _____

PLURAL NOUN _____

VERB _____

MAD LIBS®
WANTED: A FEW GOOD SUPERHEROES

Do you crave action and adventure like they were _____?
                                                TYPE OF FOOD (PLURAL)

Do you possess a power that no other _____ has, like the
                                      NOUN

ability to read the thoughts inside of people's _____?
                                                 PART OF THE BODY (PLURAL)

Do you like the idea of being known only by a secret identity, like

_____-woman or _____-man? If so, consider
     ANIMAL   NOUN

joining our team of ultra-_____ Superheroes as we covertly
                            ADJECTIVE

patrol the streets and skies around (the) _____ to keep them
                                            A PLACE

safe for all the men, women, and _____ _____
                                  PLURAL NOUN   VERB ENDING IN "ING"

there. While previous Superhero experience is not necessary, candidates

who can _____ in the face of danger while totally rocking
         VERB

a/an _____ Supersuit will be given top consideration. This is
      ADJECTIVE

a volunteer position, but we believe the _____ feeling of
                                           ADJECTIVE

satisfaction you'll get from helping the good guys triumph over all the

evil _____ will be payment enough. Does the job of a Super
      PLURAL NOUN

sound like it's for you? Then _____ today for an application!
                               VERB

Download Mad Libs today!

Join the millions of Mad Libs fans
creating wacky and wonderful
stories on our apps!